EARTHQUAKES in Action

Ewan McLeish

rosen publishing's
rosen central

New York

Published in 2009 by The Rosen Publishing Group Inc.
29 East 21st Street, New York, NY 10010

Copyright © 2009 Wayland/The Rosen Publishing Group, Inc.

First Edition

Editor: Susie Brooks
Managing Editor: Rasha Elsaeed
Designer: Tim Mayer, MayerMedia
Picture Researcher: Shelley Noronha

Library of Congress Cataloging-in-Publication Data

McLeish, Ewan, 1950-
    Earthquakes in action / Ewan McLeish. -- 1st ed.
        p. cm. -- (Natural disasters in action)
    Includes index.
    ISBN 978-1-4042-1865-9 (library binding)
    ISBN 978-1-4358-5135-1 (paperback)
    ISBN 978-1-4042-7876-9 (6-pack)
    1. Earthquakes. I. Title.
    QE534.3.M35 2008
    551.22--dc22

                        2007043366

Photo credits: Cover, 12 ©Rex Features/Sipa Press;
1, 19 ©USGS/C.E. Meyer; Bckgd 3-48 ©USGS/M. Celebi; Bckgd (panels) 4-45 ©USGS/J.K. Nakata; 4, 5, 8, 23, 26-27
©Reuters/Corbis; 6 ©Tom Bean/Corbis; 9 ©Bettmann/Corbis; 11, 13 ©Rex Features/Sipa Press; 15 ©Rex Features/KD/
Keystone U.S.A.; 16-17 ©Jim Sugar/Corbis; 18 ©Bettmann/ Corbis; 20-21 ©Kim Kulish/Corbis; 24 ©TWPhoto/Corbis;
25 ©Issei Kato/Reuters/Corbis; 28 ©ABC Ajansi/Corbis Sygma; 29 ©Louisa Gouliamaki/epa/Corbis; 30-31 ©Izmit Collection
(IZT-453)/EERC Library; 33 ©Shahpari Sohaie/ Corbis; 34 ©Morteza Nikoubazl/Reuters/Corbis; 35 ©Raheb Homvandi/
Reuters/Corbis; 36-37 ©TH-Foto/zefa/Corbis; 38 ©Goran Tomasevic/Reuters/Corbis; 40 ©Altaf Qadri/epa/ Corbis; 41 ©Mian
Khursheed/Reuters/Corbis; 42-43 ©Goran Tomasevic/Reuters/Corbis; 44 ©Alamy/ Jeremy Horner; 45 ©Issei
Kato/Reuters/Corbis

Manufactured in China

CONTENTS

When an earthquake strikes

Imagine what it is like to experience an earthquake. You feel the floor of your home start to shake beneath your feet. Plates and cups fly off shelves and pictures drop from the walls. You rush out of the door, struggling to stay upright. Things are crashing around you—you feel dazed and confused. Then you turn to your house. It is no longer there. Your street is now nothing but a ghostly pile of rubble, with friends and family buried beneath.

Real-life drama

Thousands of people around the world experience the effects of earthquakes every year. For them, the story is not imaginary—and it is only the start. How will they cope with the loss of loved ones, the lack of shelter, the threat of disease, the polluted water, their ruined crops? How will they rebuild their homes—and their lives?

A pattern emerges

A woman from a Peruvian highland town contemplates the remains of her home, destroyed in an earthquake in 2001. She and her child were lucky to survive—70 people were killed.

Earthquakes around the world have several things in common. One is that the majority of deaths and injuries are caused not by the earthquakes themselves, but by the collapse of buildings with people inside. Other casualties may be victims of the fires, landslides, or tsunamis that frequently follow earthquakes. Rescue efforts are regularly hindered by damage to infrastructure, such as roads, hospitals, and communication systems. Also, the authorities often seem unprepared to cope with the disasters when they happen.

Paying the cost

There are contrasts between these natural disasters, too. Earthquakes vary in size, or magnitude. But even earthquakes that are similar in strength may have very different results in terms of death toll and damage. For example, in 2003, an earthquake in Bam, Iran, killed more than 30,000 people (see pages 32–37). Shortly before this, a quake of equal strength hit large parts of southern California, but here, only three people lost their lives. California is a very wealthy state. Billions of dollars had been invested in constructing or strengthening buildings and bridges, so they could withstand large earth tremors.

This apartment building has completely toppled over after an earthquake in Taipei, northern Taiwan.

The will to go on

The enormous devastation that earthquakes cause can lead to acts of great bravery and kindness as local people, emergency services, and other countries work together to help stricken communities. Many of the people who survive these terrible catastrophes show tremendous courage despite the huge losses they suffer. This book looks at what we can learn that may help to reduce people's suffering in the future. We cannot stop earthquakes from happening, but we can be better prepared to minimize the damage and reduce the number of deaths and injuries that they cause.

SHAKING CITIES

There are now 200 "supercities" of more than two million people in the world. More than 40 of these are in earthquake-prone regions. Many are in poor countries where residents live in crowded streets of unstable housing. Unless building standards improve, earthquakes will continue to kill at least 10,000 people a year, with countless others left hurt or homeless.

What causes earthquakes?

The Earth's surface is constantly moving on a mass of semi-molten rock. The movement is very slow—an average of about .75 inch (2 cm) per year, the rate at which fingernails grow—so we do not usually feel it. However, the effect of this gradual movement unleashes the force of 100,000 atomic bombs every year in the form of earthquakes.

Layered Earth

To understand earthquakes, we need to know about the structure of the Earth. At the center of the planet is a dense core, made up of the metals iron and nickel. Around this is the mantle, a massive layer of super-heated rock that seems solid but actually flows very slowly as deeper, hotter material rises through it in streams called convection currents. Earth's outermost layer—the crust—is a thinner covering of solid rock on which the oceans and continents lie.

The crust is not a continuous layer —it is divided into large sections called tectonic plates. Those below the sea are called oceanic plates. They form little more than a skin on the surface of the planet, somewhere between 2.5–6 miles (4–10 km) thick. The plates that support land are called continental plates; they are thicker—between 18.5–62 miles (30–100 km)—but less dense than the oceanic plates. Both types of plate move slowly over the face of the globe, powered by the currents in the mantle.

The San Andreas Fault in California represents the boundary between an oceanic and a continental plate. Differences to the left and right of the fault line show that the two sections of land are moving very slowly past each other in opposite directions.

When plates collide

Along the West Coast, the massive oceanic Pacific plate slides slowly north past the North American plate, along a boundary known as the San Andreas Fault. As these plates move, they catch on each other. The edges gradually buckle until the stress can no longer be contained. Then the plates suddenly lurch past each other by a distance of several yards, releasing huge amounts of energy and creating violent tremors, or earthquakes.

In other parts of the world, plates either move apart or meet head on. Where two different kinds of plate meet, the thinner, denser oceanic plate pushes its way under the continental plate in a process known as subduction. This creates enormous pressures, enough to melt the rock that is being pushed down, and may result in volcanic activity, earthquakes, or tsunamis.

DEADLY WAVES

In December 2004, an underwater earthquake along the boundary between the huge Asian and Indian plates triggered a giant tsunami, whose towering waves killed more than a quarter of a million people in the Indian Ocean region.

Deadly pattern

About 95 percent of all the world's earthquakes occur along plate boundaries. These exist, for example, along the west coast of South America and to the east of the landmass of Asia, passing through Japan and Papua New Guinea. All countries positioned over plate boundaries, or fault lines, have been involved in major earthquakes.

The purple areas on this map show the locations of some of the worst earthquakes in recent history. The black lines represent plate boundaries.

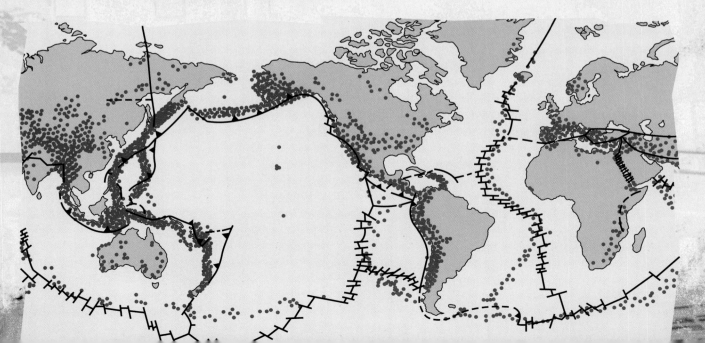

Measuring earthquakes

The study of earthquakes is called seismology. Seismologists (scientists who work in this field) can measure the intensity of a tremor under the ground using specialist equipment. They can also work out exactly where an earthquake began.

SEISMIC WAVES

There are different types of seismic waves. Body waves travel through the Earth. They are divided into primary (P) waves and secondary (S) waves. Primary waves are faster and cause vertical (up-and-down) shaking of the ground. Secondary waves cause sideways movement. However, it is the second main kind of wave, the slower surface waves, that do the most damage. These can travel only along the Earth's surface, but they are capable of producing very large vibrations in rocks and soils.

Profile of an earthquake

The point at which a sudden movement between two plates occurs is called the focus. This is usually quite deep within the Earth's crust, perhaps 12–18 miles (20–30 km) or more. The sudden jolt cracks the crust and sends out a series of rippling seismic waves, which spread upward and outward. The point at which they reach the Earth's surface is called the epicenter. The tremors created may last for a few seconds or several minutes. They can travel for hundreds of miles at terrifying speeds before losing their destructive energy. During that time, they may cause great devastation and loss of life. The main shock is often followed by a series of aftershocks, usually of lesser intensity. These may add to the damage already suffered in the initial shock.

This woman in Taipei, Taiwan, is taking readings from a modern seismometer. On the day this picture was taken, an earth tremor of magnitude 6.3, shown by the horizontal lines, was registered.

Power to destroy

The magnitude of an earthquake is usually given as a number between 1 and 10 on a measure known as the Richter scale. It is recorded on a device called a seismometer, which measures the size, duration (length of time), and frequency of the vibrations. Each point on the Richter scale represents an increase in size of the earthquake by a factor of 10. This means that a size 8 tremor is 10 times greater than a 7, and so on.

Earthquakes that do very serious damage usually measure somewhere between 6.5 and 7.5 on the Richter scale, but smaller earthquakes can be just as devastating, depending on many different factors. As we shall see, these include the closeness of the epicenter to areas of high population, the local geology, and the type of building construction in the region affected.

In 1906, a huge earthquake destroyed much of San Francisco. It is clear that, even 100 years ago, some buildings were better able to withstand earth tremors than others.

THE RICHTER SCALE

RATING	NUMBER PER YEAR	TYPICAL EFFECTS
Less than 3.4	800,000	Detected only by seismometers
3.5–4.2	30,000	Just about noticeable indoors
4.3–4.8	4,800	Windows rattle
4.9–5.4	1,400	Dishes break, open doors swing
5.5–6.1	500	Slight damage to buildings, plaster cracks, bricks fall
6.2–6.9	100	Much damage to buildings, chimneys fall, houses move on foundations
7.0–7.3	15	Serious damage, bridges twist, walls fracture, buildings may collapse
7.4–7.9	4	Great damage, most buildings collapse
Greater than 8	One every 5–10 years	Total damage, surface waves seen, objects thrown in air

MEXICO CITY, MEXICO, 1985

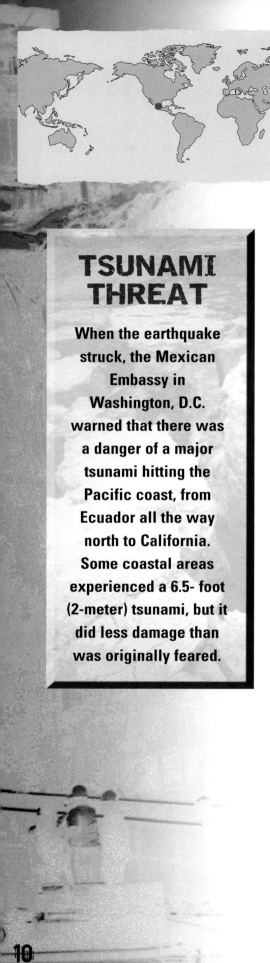

On September 19, 1985, a massive earthquake occurred 40 miles (65 km) off the Pacific (west) coast of Mexico. Measuring 8.1 on the Richter scale, it was the strongest recorded earthquake ever to hit the region. Tremors were experienced over an area of 318,450 sq. mi. (825,000 sq. km)—almost half the extent of the country. The quake was felt as far away as Houston (745 mi. or 1,200 km to the north) and in Guatemala City (620 mi. or 1,000 km to the south).

Instant destruction

The earthquake struck at 7:17 a.m. Damage was widespread. On the Pacific coast, part of a mountain broke away, falling onto farm laborers who were just starting work. At the beach resort of Playa Azul, 30 people died and 150 were injured when hotels collapsed. Some inland industrial towns were also badly hit. Then, two minutes later, more than 217 miles (350 km) away in the very center of Mexico, catastrophe struck the capital. Destruction in Mexico City made this one of the most devastating earthquakes of the twentieth century.

Crushed capital

The earthquake shook the city for three horrifying minutes. For many residents, this seemed like an eternity. Early estimates said that hundreds of people had been killed, but it was soon clear that the number would be in the thousands, perhaps tens of thousands. Clouds of dust hung over the city center, and broken glass and great chunks of cement littered the desolated streets. A strong smell of gas began to fill the air as gas mains ruptured. Several high-rise hotels had collapsed entirely, as had a section of the city's huge medical center. Many buildings were on fire, the blazes fueled by gas from the shattered pipes.

TSUNAMI THREAT

When the earthquake struck, the Mexican Embassy in Washington, D.C. warned that there was a danger of a major tsunami hitting the Pacific coast, from Ecuador all the way north to California. Some coastal areas experienced a 6.5- foot (2-meter) tsunami, but it did less damage than was originally feared.

Communications down

Telephone lines were ripped down and a communications tower was burning, which meant television broadcasts had to be sent via neighboring Guatemala. Reports began to emerge that a third of all buildings in the city had been damaged or destroyed. The underground railroad system had failed and hundreds of people were trapped in its tunnels.

EYEWITNESS

❝ The walls were swaying back and forth so much we thought they were going to collapse. My mother hurried me and my brothers outside into the street; it was not easy to walk. The shaking was more intense and the ground rolled for over two minutes. ❞

Gicela, 16, a resident of Mexico City

Cranes assist in recovery operations after the earthquake in Mexico City. The overall damage took years to repair.

DISASTER DAYS

SEPTEMBER 19, 1985
7:17 a.m. Huge undersea earthquake occurs 40 mi. (65 km) off west coast of Mexico.

7:19 a.m. Shockwaves hit Mexico City, 217 mi. (350 km) inland.

7:22 a.m. Parts of Mexico City are almost totally destroyed; thousands are killed instantly.

8:30 a.m. Much of Mexico City is ablaze; thousands of people are trapped on underground railroads. Rescue services begin to take action.

9:30 a.m. U.S. Mexican Embassy issues a tsunami warning along western South and North American coasts; only limited damage occurs.

SEPTEMBER 22
Huge aftershock hits Mexico City and other regions, causing further damage and hindering rescue operations.

MARCH 1986
Lack of government action brings local groups together to begin rebuilding houses on the sites of destroyed homes.

SEPTEMBER 1990
Local reconstruction continues; many public buildings are strengthened; earthquake drills are in place.

SEPTEMBER 1999
Earthquake measuring 7.4 on the Richter scale hits Mexico City; one person is killed as a result.

DANGER ZONE

The region where the earthquake originated is a subduction zone. Here, the oceanic Cocos plate dives beneath the continental land mass of the North American plate, creating the most active "thrust" fault in the Western Hemisphere. As a result of activity in this zone, Mexico experienced 42 earthquakes measuring over 7 on the Richter scale in the twentieth century—a rate of nearly one every two years.

Fatal aftershock

The worst was not over—36 hours after the main earthquake, a massive aftershock struck Mexico City. This was almost as severe as the first tremor, magnifying the damage and causing fresh panic among the capital's inhabitants. Casualties now numbered tens of thousands, and 6,000 buildings in the city had crumbled, including hotels, hospitals, homes, schools, and industrial centers. Communications between the Mexican capital and the outside world were disrupted for days.

Rescue efforts

A huge rescue operation was well underway by the time the aftershock struck. The government had appealed for blood donors, and 10,000 police and troops were patrolling the rubble-strewn streets to try to prevent looting. Rescue efforts continued—survivors were still being hauled out of the debris a week after the disaster. Among the most remarkable rescues was that of 58 newborn babies, pulled from the wreckage of two large hospitals three days after the earthquake struck.

These rescuers in Mexico City seem dwarfed by the tangle of wreckage that was once a modern urban center. Not only were buildings destroyed, but also streets were blocked by debris, hampering the efforts of the emergency services.

With their powerful sense of smell, specially trained dogs are often used to help search for survivors who are buried under piles of rubble.

International aid

An appeal for foreign aid brought rapid responses from Latin America, the U.S., Canada, and Europe. However, there was strong criticism from rescue workers about the lack of any coordinated plan by the government of Mexico to cope with a disaster of this size. Eight days after the event, city residents began protests against the government's slowness in helping the thousands of people made homeless. The following day, the Mexican president, Miguel de la Madrid, called a meeting to draw up a reconstruction program and to decide how to assist the 300,000 people affected by the disaster.

SINGING FOR SURVIVORS

Among those who lost members of their family in the disaster was the Spanish singer, Placido Domingo, (one of the famous "Three Tenors"), who grew up in Mexico. He helped with the rescue effort and later staged a benefit concert that raised $2 million for the stricken capital and its people.

TOUGH TOWER

One building, the 44-floor Torre Latinoamericana, remained almost totally undamaged in contrast to many more modern buildings that collapsed. The building is a symmetrical steel-framed structure, specifically designed to withstand earthquakes. It has 200 piles (vertical foundations) extending 115 feet (35 meters) through the soft clay to the topmost layer of stable rock beneath.

Shaky ground

Why did the earthquake cause so much destruction so far away from its epicenter? After all, areas much nearer the epicenter, such as the coastal resorts of Acapulco and Zihuatanejo, suffered much less damage. The reason lies partly in the geology of Mexico City. The city sits in a broad river basin formed about 30 million years ago. Lava (molten rock) thrown out from nearby volcanoes blocked the entrance to the basin and created a huge lake—Lake Texcoco. As the capital expanded, much of the lake was drained, leaving the world's most densely populated city located largely on soft clay. The layers in the clay made the seismic waves of the earthquake as much as 50 times stronger—a phenomenon known as resonance. In addition, the vibrations caused the subsoils (layers of soil beneath the surface) to behave like liquids in a process called liquefaction. As a result, some buildings literally sank into the ground.

The buildings in the highest damage category were mainly medium-height structures with six to fifteen floors. These buildings vibrated with the same frequency as the subsoils. The resonance experienced here made the overall size of the vibration dramatically bigger, and therefore increased the damage. Many other buildings that collapsed were simply not designed or constructed well enough to withstand an earthquake of such force.

Learning for the future

Several important lessons were learned from the terrible destruction of Mexico City. It was clear that some types of structure survived the earthquake better than others. A flexible building, which might have withstood the shock on its own, failed if it was held on either side by more rigid, lower buildings. Damage often occurred where two swaying buildings came into contact. Corner buildings were also more likely to fall. Better planning could avoid some of these problems in the future.

The new Torre Mayor tower in the center of Mexico City is a demonstration of state-of-the-art earthquake protection. It has giant shock absorbers that are designed to withstand quakes in excess of 8.5 on the Richter scale.

Since 1985, the Mexican government has funded a sophisticated early-warning system. This sends warning messages to Mexico City electronically from sensors in the coastal region of Guerrero, where the 1985 earthquake began. When seismic activity occurs, sirens automatically sound, giving city residents up to a minute's warning that a quake may be coming. Systems like this could save thousands of lives.

The final death toll resulting from the 1985 earthquake will never be known—thousands of bodies were never found. Official figures stated that there were 10,000 deaths, but many residents believe that up to ten times this number of people were killed.

QUAKE COSTS

- 10,000 deaths reported (actual figure probably 60,000–100,000)
- 50,000 people injured
- 250,000–300,000 people made homeless
- Total cost of damage: $12.5 billion

SAN FRANCISCO, U.S.A., 1989

In the late afternoon of October 17, 1989, the ground shook across northern California. A major earthquake had struck the region of Mount Loma Prieta, Santa Cruz, 62 miles (100 kilometers) south of San Francisco. The "Loma Prieta," as the quake came to be known, caused severe damage in the city of Oakland, the San Francisco peninsular, San Francisco itself, and areas closer to the epicenter around Santa Cruz. Tremors were felt as far away as Los Angeles and Nevada, 375 miles (600 kilometers) to the south.

ROCKY PAST

San Francisco is used to earthquakes. It lies on the San Andreas Fault, where the Pacific plate grinds past the North American plate, and it has experienced repeated tremors over the past 50 years. The worst by far was a 1906 earthquake, which devastated much of the city. More than a quarter of a million people were made homeless after fires raged out of control, and 700 people died.

From excitement to disaster

At 5:00 p.m. on the day of the earthquake, there was excitement in the San Francisco Bay Area. The Bay's two Major League Baseball teams, the Oakland Athletics and the San Francisco Giants, were about to play their third game of the World Series. Many people had left work early in order to watch the game on television at home or in local bars. As we shall see, this seemingly unconnected event was to save many hundreds of lives.

The earthquake struck at 5:04 p.m. It lasted for 15 seconds and measured 7.1 on the Richter scale. Early estimates suggested that nine people had been killed, and several hundred more had been injured. Officials reported "unbelievable damage to infrastructure" with fires, landslides, shattered buildings, and gaping cracks in roads. Then reports came in that the two-tier Bay Bridge and the Nimitz Freeway, connecting San Francisco and Oakland, had both partially collapsed.

By far the more serious of the two was the damage to the Cypress Street Viaduct on the Nimitz Freeway. It soon became clear that the upper part of the bridge had fallen in, crushing cars on the lower deck. A total of 42 people lost their lives on this stretch of road, accounting for two-thirds of all deaths caused by the earthquake. A 52-foot (16-meter) section of the San Francisco-Oakland Bay Bridge had also collapsed, causing two cars to fall to the deck below. Here there was one fatality.

Disaster strikes the Nimitz Freeway connecting San Francisco and Oakland during the earthquake of 1989.

SHOCK IN THE SEA

The Loma Prieta earthquake triggered a 4.2-foot (1.3-m) high tsunami in Monterey Bay, as well as a huge undersea landslide. The sea level dropped 3 ft. (1 m) at Santa Cruz as water rushed out of the harbor. The waves took 20 minutes to hit Monterey, 22 mi. (35 km) to the south.

Life saver

What about the World Series game that was due to start at 5:30 on the evening of the earthquake? Fans actually waiting to see the game at Candlestick Park ran onto the pitch as the stadium swayed. No one was hurt. But the tens of thousands of people who had left work early to see the game on television had even greater reason to be grateful. Hundreds of them would normally have been sitting in long traffic jams on the freeways between San Francisco and Oakland. As it was, the Nimitz Freeway was relatively clear of traffic when its massive upper deck came crashing down.

Ghostly fires

As night fell, damage to power lines and generating stations plunged San Francisco into darkness. Power was only fully restored three days later. Emergency telephone services were interrupted as fire broke out in the 911 center. Citizens therefore had to rely on fire alarms to alert emergency teams. At least 27 fires were already raging across the city, including a major blaze in apartment buildings in the Marina district in San Francisco. These apartments had been built on rubble and debris resulting from the 1906 earthquake. Now it seemed the legacy had come back to haunt them as this unstable ground turned to mud in the tremors, swallowing the buildings up.

Crowds move onto the baseball diamond at Candlestick Park as the stadium sways in the earthquake.

Buildings lie damaged in the Marina district of San Francisco. While some structures collapsed and burned, others sank into the muddy ground.

Assessing the damage

The Loma Prieta was the second biggest earthquake ever to hit the U.S. Two days after the disaster, an idea of the scale of the event began to emerge. Damaged buildings included the Main Library, the Hall of Justice, the Opera House, Candlestick Park stadium, and the airport. Insurance experts said the earthquake was the "sixth costliest disaster" in the country's history. On the following day, scientists located the epicenter of the earthquake near Mount Loma Prieta. They reported fissures (cracks) hundreds of yards long and up to half a yard wide.

Now it was also clear that many of the damaged houses were in an extremely dangerous condition. The city's mayor informed devastated residents that they had just 15 minutes to enter their homes to collect belongings before the buildings were demolished by the authorities.

WIDESPREAD DAMAGE

San Francisco and its surrounding areas were not the only places badly hit. The city of Oakland, on the other side of the freeways that had so tragically collapsed, was also severely damaged. Here, 42 people lost their lives and many more were injured. Closer to the epicenter, the sleepy town of Santa Cruz itself was nearly flattened. Six people were killed and another 600 were injured.

Aiding recovery

On October 22, five days after the disaster, 20,000 people gathered in Golden Gate Park to hear the San Francisco Symphony Orchestra play a benefit concert for those affected by the earthquake. The U.S. Navy carrier, U.S.S. *Peleliu*, became one of three ships to give temporary accommodation to those who had lost their homes. Two days later, Congress began to debate an "earthquake relief bill." One Wisconsin congressman complained that Californians were too wealthy to need financial aid. Nevertheless, on October 26, President George Bush (Sr.) signed a $3.45 billion earthquake relief package for California.

The postponed game between the Oakland Athletics and the San Francisco Giants, which had indirectly saved so many lives, was played ten days after the earthquake struck. Many thought the World Series should have been canceled as a mark of respect for those who had lost their lives.

QUAKE COSTS

- 63 deaths
- 3,500 people injured
- 12,000 people made homeless
- Total cost: $8.7 billion

EYEWITNESS

❝ If they had not been so parsimonious [cost-conscious], a mile of Interstate 880 [the Nimitz Freeway] might not have been swatted down by an earthquake it should have ridden out easily. ❞

Architect Allen Temko, *San Francisco Chronicle*

A question of cost

Compared to many earthquakes of similar size in other countries, the number of deaths from the Loma Prieta was low. Despite this, the company responsible for transportation in the region was attacked for being inefficient, understaffed, and lacking in research funds.

The transportation company undertook a program of so-called retrofitting over the next ten years, in which more than 2,000 bridges were carefully strengthened to withstand the impact of future earthquakes. The cost of retrofitting was $4–5 billion, money that some groups said should have gone toward improving transportation systems in the region generally, rather than into bridge strengthening.

The repaired San Francisco-Oakland Bay Bridge reopened on November 17, 1989. The chief engineer on the project estimated that the pressure to the bridge from the earthquake had been more than the force needed to launch the space shuttle!

EYEWITNESS

❝ After you see all those things—the crack in the Bay Bridge, the Cypress coming down—that's like a Third World country [LEDC] and we can't have that in the U.S. Traffic is important—but safety comes first. ❞

Andrew Chen, regular commuter, San Francisco Bay Area

KOBE, JAPAN, 1995

The port of Kobe, on the Japanese island of Honshu, is a wealthy city of some 1.5 million people. Tuesday, January 17, 1995 started just like any other day. Even before 6:00 a.m., many people were up cooking breakfast or on their way to work. This was to cost many their lives. At 5:46 a.m., an earthquake measuring 7.2 on the Richter scale struck Japan. The epicenter was only about 20 miles (32 kilometers) offshore from Kobe, directly below the island of Awajisima.

A city paralyzed

The national television station, NHK, immediately began broadcasting pictures of a devastated metropolis. Hundreds of people were trapped under flattened buildings, and the elevated section of the Hanshin Expressway, connecting the nearby city of Osaka with Kobe, collapsed in three places.

One collapsed section extended for a third of a mile. A bus was left hanging and 50 cars were thrown over the edge. Trains flipped on their sides and one train station actually rolled over, crushing vehicles in its parking lot. The supposedly indestructible track of the Shinkansen bullet train broke in eight places. Fortunately, the first train of the morning had not yet left for the city center.

Fire was spreading quickly through many parts of the city, started by overturned gas burners belonging to people cooking their breakfast, as well as by broken gas pipes. Firefighters were powerless to stop the blazes, because the impact had damaged water mains and rubble blocked the roads. In addition, much of Kobe's electrical cabling was brought down, so the emergency services had no power. Tragically, more than 500 people who had survived the initial earthquake died in fires, trapped in their homes.

DISTANT DANGER

Japan lies on the intersection of three tectonic plates—the Pacific, the Eurasian, and the Philippine. Movements in the Earth's crust mean that earthquakes here are common. Kobe is located farther from the plates' meeting point than most Japanese cities, and was therefore thought to be less at risk. The devastating effect of the 1995 earthquake was partly due to the unexpected closeness of the epicenter to the city.

Evacuation

Meanwhile, thousands more people had fled into the streets, wrapped in bedding, afraid that aftershocks would follow the main earthquake. This was the middle of winter; temperatures were below freezing and 300,000 people were now homeless. Schools, town halls, and even city parks became emergency shelters. But lack of power, blankets, water, and medical supplies, as well as severe overcrowding, meant that conditions were wretched. Tens of thousands of people picked up what they could and set out on foot for the city of Osaka, 19 miles (30 km) away.

QUAKE COSTS

- 6,433 deaths
- 27,000 people injured
- 300,000 people made homeless
- Cost of damage: about $145 billion

The western part of Kobe city lies devastated in this photograph of January 1995, after fires burned through blocks of houses following the earthquake.

Unprepared

Because the western part of the country was thought to be less seismically active than the east, Kobe city was less prepared for earthquakes than many other Japanese cities at the time. In Tokyo, for example, a devastating earthquake in 1923 had killed 100,000 people. Here, over a quarter of all homes now kept emergency supplies and the authorities regularly carried out drills to test people's readiness for a major disaster. But in Osaka, less than 3 percent of households kept emergency provisions, and in Kobe, there were no drills by emergency services or the military. In addition, while planners and designers had concentrated on making public and commercial buildings earthquake resistant, ordinary homes were less well protected.

EYEWITNESS

❝ We're partly to blame because many of us have not prepared for earthquakes. But everyone here is surprised that we've had so little help. Many of us had to watch our homes burn down with not a fireman in sight. ❞

Yoshio Miyoshi, Kobe survivor

In this scene, a year after the Kobe earthquake, reconstruction is well underway. However, poorer parts of the city took longer to rebuild.

These Japanese children are among thousands of people who gathered in a park in Kobe five years after the disaster to remember those who died. Mourners lit homemade candles in bamboo holders, which were laid out in the shape of the number 17—the date when the earthquake happened.

Steady recovery

Four days after the earthquake, food and water shipments finally arrived at some of the large shelters. Running water became available in some regions of the city. Tractors and cranes began working around the clock to dig out survivors and bodies still buried in the debris. The government made an offer to build 7,000 new houses, and low-interest loans were made available to desperate homeowners, many of whom were still paying mortgages on their ruined houses.

Within five years, Kobe was completely rebuilt and now there is little sign of the event that devastated the city. But some people have questioned whether lessons from the quake have been learned. While gleaming new towers cluster along Osaka Bay, many of the homes that have been rebuilt are prefabricated or made with cheap materials, especially in the poorer areas of the city. Even ten years later, people who had been forced to borrow heavily to rebuild their homes and businesses were still dismally overwhelmed with debt. And few can forget that in the disaster of 1995, many buildings that were "earthquake proof" sank into the ground or simply fell over as the tremors caused liquefaction of the soft subsoils.

EYEWITNESS

❝ Right after the Kobe quake, most (local) governments got serious about disaster prevention. But their enthusiasm is tapering off. This country is spending billions of yen on quake prevention. But we can and must do more. ❞

Tsuneo Katayama, National Research Institute for Earthquake and Disaster Prevention

25

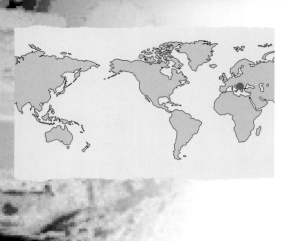

IZMIT, TURKEY, 1999

The city of Izmit lies in a heavily populated industrial area of northwestern Turkey. Most of its residents were asleep at 3:02 a.m. on August 17, 1999, when a devastating earthquake struck. The quake measured 7.4 on the Richter scale and lasted for 45 seconds. In that brief moment, more than 15,000 people died and 300,000 people lost their homes, their possessions, their families, and their friends.

EYEWITNESS

❝ This is the biggest natural disaster I have ever witnessed… May Allah help our state and our people. ❞

Bulent Ecevit, Turkish prime minister

Death in the night

As is so often the case with natural disasters, early reports of the severity of this earthquake were pitifully inaccurate. Some said that 100 people had died and maybe another 500 were injured. But as day dawned, the full extent of the damage began to emerge. Many multistory buildings had collapsed, burying their sleeping inhabitants beneath hundreds of tons of rubble. To make matters worse, an oil refinery on the outskirts of the city had caught fire and was blazing out of control, diverting fire crews who were desperately needed elsewhere.

Cities as far away as Istanbul, 62 miles (100 km) to the west, and the Turkish capital Ankara, 124 miles (200 km) to the southeast, felt the ground shudder. In the capital, a crisis center was rapidly set up to coordinate emergency efforts. But the earthquake had also severely damaged power cables, and telephone lines and communications were disabled. State radio began broadcasting information as people woke to a day of tragic news. One report said that vehicles on the main Istanbul-Ankara highway had slammed into each other as the earthquake struck.

Daylight devastation

By 8:00 a.m., most survivors in the region of the earthquake were keeping away from their potentially dangerous houses and listening for news. In Istanbul they gathered in groups with their neighbors, afraid that aftershocks would bring more devastation. Three shocks were experienced in half an hour, but the better-designed buildings in this city merely "swayed gracefully."

In Izmit itself, the scene was very different. Television pictures started to show dazed and bleeding people being rescued from the rubble. As darkness approached on the first day, the death toll rose to 2,000, but it was clear that this was only the start of a long and painful recovery operation.

A residential area near Izmit lies in ruins after the 1999 earthquake. Different standards of building meant that some apartment buildings collapsed completely while others in the same street suffered much less damage.

MAKING WAVES

The earthquake occurred in a region where the North Anatolian Fault is squeezed to the south and southwest by the surrounding Arabian, Eurasian, and African plates. Not only did the quake destroy Izmit and severely damage several other cities, including Istanbul, Adapazari, and Gölcük, it also threw up a 20-foot (6-meter) tsunami that devastated the resort of Degirmendere.

Ongoing rescue

Throughout the night of August 18, rescue workers and those who had escaped the destruction continued to search for survivors. Many rescuers were digging through debris with their bare hands. That night, millions of people in the region, the most heavily populated in Turkey, stayed out in the open.

By now it was clear that, even for an earthquake-prone country, this was a disaster of enormous proportions. Appeals were made for international help to locate and rescue survivors still trapped in the rubble. Offers of rescue teams came pouring in from Israel, Germany, Japan, the U.S., the U.K., and Russia. The following night and day would be crucial. The weather was hot, and the people who were still trapped had little oxygen and were also in danger of dehydration. Previous experience of earthquakes in the region showed that the chance of anyone surviving longer than 24 hours in these conditions was slim. Official reports suggested that 10,000 people were still buried under the collapsed city.

Residents celebrate momentarily as a young boy is pulled from the wreckage.

Grief mixed with anger

Two days after the earthquake, the death toll stood at 6,866, but the number missing had not reduced. People complained that the rescue operation was inefficient. Tent cities were being put up for homeless survivors, but food and clean water supplies were dwindling. Outbreaks of cholera, a disease caused by contaminated water, were reported in some areas of Istanbul. Crowds mobbed a convoy of bread trucks in Izmit, where now it was estimated that at least 76,000 buildings had collapsed. Despite the aid pouring in from abroad, many people said they had been left to hunt for missing relatives unaided in the rubble of their own homes.

Meanwhile, the Tupras oil refinery in Izmit was still ablaze, sending thousands of tons of dark, toxic smoke into the atmosphere. People started to express concern about the environmental effects of the disaster. Anger was also growing in other areas. Turkey had been experiencing an economic boom in recent years. It was becoming clear that many buildings that had been constructed in this rapidly growing industrial area were of a poor standard. They were not built to withstand this kind of shock, even though it was known that Turkey lies on an active fault line.

A British newspaper ran the headline, *"Corruption kills people—not earthquakes."* Reporters claimed it was easy to find officials who could be bribed to allow poor housing to be built. Another paper was less critical. It said that Turkey's poor could not afford to meet proper building regulations, and that it was the responsibility of richer countries to help with long-term investment. With so much damage to power lines, rail links, and water supplies, the long-term effects on Turkey's economy were also in question.

A firefighting aircraft attempts to put out the flames of the burning Tupras oil refinery, amid fears that the fire could spread to residential areas. Some 1,300 people, mainly employees and soldiers, battled to stop the blaze that set alight five of the plant's 30 oil tanks overnight.

QUAKE COSTS

- Officially 15,000–17,000 deaths (probably nearer 40,000)
- About 40,000 people injured
- 300,000 people made homeless
- Total cost of damage: $12-23 billion

Glimmers of hope

Alongside the anger and the grief, there were some stories of amazing resilience and survival. A full 100 hours after the earthquake hit, at least five children and a 95-year-old woman were pulled alive from the wreckage.

However, a week after the earthquake, other concerns began to emerge. Experts warned about the long-term psychological effects on the survivors. The rescue operation began to shift from finding trapped people to helping the men, women, and children who had been left to rebuild their lives. Many people would never know where their lost loved ones were buried, and this made it more difficult for the survivors to grieve.

Three months later, 6,000 prefabricated houses were opened to survivors, the first of a planned 32,000. On August 17, 2000, a year after the earthquake, millions of Turks gathered in public squares and cemeteries to remember the dead. More than 42,000 new homes were now under construction.

EYEWITNESS

❝ The most difficult things to cope with after a tragedy are the feelings that you have survived, while others have not. ❞

Lorraine Sheer, psychologist, Royal Free Hospital, London

Warning signs

Could the earthquake have been foreseen? For many years, scientists had noticed a pattern of earthquakes moving across northern Turkey from east to west along the North Anatolian fault line. It seemed that each quake was somehow triggering the next, five, ten, or twenty years later. Based on this theory, a U.S. geologist predicted that the next big quake would be in the Izmit area. Less than two years later, he was proved correct. But his warnings had been largely ignored, even though they were widely reported in national newspapers at the time. Now the data suggests that the next major earthquake will be centered on a city of 14 million people—the city of Istanbul itself.

A safer future?

Could the devastation of 1999 have been avoided? Most of the collapsed multistory buildings were believed to be highly earthquake resistant. In fact, for various reasons, they were not. First, the buildings did not meet the "design requirements" they were supposed to; in addition, they were poorly constructed from inadequate materials. Furthermore, many buildings were knowingly built on or close to active fault lines. The Turkish prime minister said that the quake had been "a warning" to prepare for natural disasters before they strike. He said that special search-and-rescue teams had been expanded and regulations to improve poor building structures had been put in place. Only time will tell if enough has been done to avert any future disaster.

In this picture a mosque stands undamaged among a sea of rubble in the town on Gölcük, 62 miles (100 km) northeast of Izmit. Older buildings are often better constructed, and therefore more resilient to earthquakes than more recent structures, which may have been hastily built from inferior or inappropriate materials.

BAM, IRAN, 2003

On December 26, 2003, an earthquake measuring 6.5 on the Richter scale hit the historic city of Bam in southeastern Iran. The destruction was almost total—over 80 percent of the city's ancient mud-brick buildings crumbled with the trembling of the ground. The earthquake struck at 5:28 a.m., with its epicenter close to the city. As in the disaster at Izmit, Turkey, thousands of people were crushed to death in their beds.

Total devastation

The mud-brick conctructions collapsed quickly, leaving no life-saving air pockets for those buried. Many of the people who escaped being crushed were suffocated instead. It was almost as though a giant bulldozer had gone out of control and reduced everything to rubble and choking dust. In places, half-demolished buildings tottered on the edges of mountains of debris, ready to collapse completely. Every parked car had its roof squashed flat. The impact of the quake was so huge that school buildings up to 55 miles (90 km) away were damaged and unsafe. In the littered streets of Bam, there was inconsolable grief as people wept next to bodies of loved ones.

Call for help

Iran's leader, President Khatami, spoke of a "national tragedy." He urged all Iranians to help the earthquake victims. A large relief operation was immediately put underway, involving the army, volunteer groups, local rescue teams, and the general public. Emergency centers were set up in makeshift buildings, where rescue workers desperately tried to care for the tens of thousands of people who had been injured. Two of the city's hospitals had collapsed, killing and wounding many staff and increasing the pressure on remaining medical facilities. In addition, this was a desert city in full winter. Temperatures at night plummeted to well below zero—a serious danger to those trapped in collapsed buildings or left without shelter.

QUAKE COSTS

- 41,000 deaths
- About 30,00 people injured
- 80,000 people made homeless
- Cost of rebuilding homes: $2 billion
- Cost of lost historic buildings/artefacts: impossible to value

A human tragedy

Six days after the earthquake, all hope of finding survivors was lost. The death toll now exceeded 30,000. Many survivors had left the city to stay with families elsewhere. Those 20,000 or so who remained were living under tents in the freezing conditions. The Iranian authorities were looking for sites to set up more organized camps while people waited for homes to be rebuilt. However, many of the survivors refused to leave the ruins of their old houses, where many of their loved ones were still buried.

This photograph, taken across the whole city of Bam shortly after the earthquake, shows the level of devastation. The fragile buildings meant that the damage was much greater than the size of the quake might have suggested.

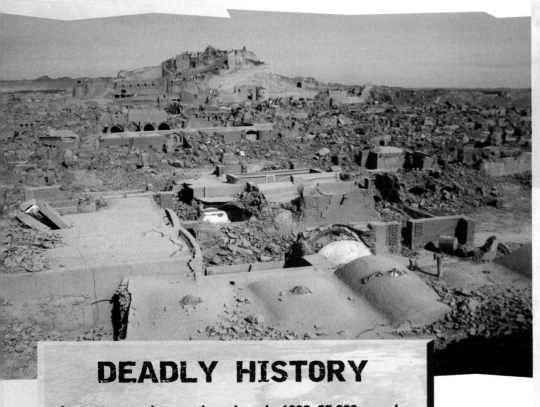

DEADLY HISTORY

Iran was used to earthquakes. In 1990, 35,000 people had died in the country's worst recorded natural disaster. Since that time, tremors had claimed a further 17,600 lives. No one tried to understate the severity of the 2003 event. The death toll was instantly put at more than 15,000.

DISASTER DAYS

DECEMBER 26, 2003
5:28 a.m. Earthquake of magnitude 6.5 occurs close to the ancient city of Bam.

10:30 a.m. Emergency centers are set up to cope with dying and injured people.

7:30 p.m. Rescue attempts speed up to prevent trapped survivors dying of cold.

DECEMBER 27
International rescue teams start to arrive.

JANUARY 1, 2004
Expectations of finding survivors reach zero. Tented communities are set up.

JANUARY 3
Last survivor, a 97-year-old woman, is pulled to safety. She requests a cup of tea!

JUNE 2004
World Bank approves a huge loan to the government of Iran to help restore living conditions and infrastructure.

DECEMBER 2004
Shops and businesses spring up along roadsides; only 5 percent of houses have been rebuilt; 24,000 children are at school in temporary buildings.

DECEMBER 2006
Some progress has been made but rebuilding work is slow; many people are still living in poor conditions in temporary homes.

Coping with chaos

The Bam authorities appeared to be coping well. Water points were sufficient to prevent large lines from developing, and food and mineral water were being distributed efficiently. The threat of major outbreaks of diseases such as cholera seemed to have been contained. However, much of the distribution of foreign aid was chaotic, particularly that of clothes and other essentials for everyday living.

An accident waiting to happen?

This earthquake was a double tragedy. Not only had tens of thousands of people died, but also the great architectural and historic features of an ancient city had been destroyed in moments. Bam was on UNESCO's list of World Heritage Sites, which includes the Taj Mahal, the Great Wall of China, and the Galapagos Islands. But Bam's ancient buildings had not been built to withstand earthquakes. The 2,000-year-old mud-brick citadel (fortress), along with other buildings constructed of the same material, had simply collapsed like flimsy card houses.

A religious leader prays at a mass grave, while excavations of additional burial chambers go on around him.

A truck is all that prevents this building from toppling further. Both are now beyond repair.

The more modern buildings had fared little better. Efforts to bring industrial development to what was an undeveloped agricultural area had caused a large increase in population. The resulting housing shortage had led people to build cheap, unstable homes, or to tack on extra floors to existing houses. Some buildings had collapsed even before the earthquake.

In addition, houses in earthquake-prone regions should have lightweight, sloping roofs, fixed together at close intervals. In Bam, there were mainly heavy, flat roofs made of concrete reinforced with steel beams. The traditional brick arches on which the roofs stood were unable to support their weight as the walls began to shake. The roofs collapsed, crushing everything beneath them. The use of wood in construction could have saved thousands of lives. Wood, however, is in short supply in regions like this.

A new beginning

By early January 2004, the talk was of reconstruction—and in the longer term—of building an Iran where structures would be better able to withstand earthquakes. The 2,000-year-old Arg-e-Bam citadel would be reconstructed with the help of organizations such as the United Nations, but the Bam of the future is likely to have a very different skyline from the one that so suddenly disappeared.

In 2004, the World Bank approved a $220 million loan to the government of Iran for a project to help restore the living conditions of communities in Bam. The four-year project was designed to help build housing in Bam with improved safety standards, and to restore telecommunications and transportation links. Now, more than halfway through the project, little progress appears to have been made. Relief work has dwindled and rebuilding is going slowly.

LOST HISTORY

Bam used to be one of Iran's most popular tourist attractions. During the Safavid Dynasty (1501–1736), the city was surrounded by rampart walls with 38 towers. It had 9,000–13,000 residents and was a popular pilgrimage site for Muslims. It was also an important trading center on the famous "Silk Road," along which merchants brought exotic goods from the Far East to Europe. Bam declined in the early eighteenth century and was abandoned in 1932. But in 1953, Iranian authorities began to restore the city's ancient quarter, attracting thousands of new visitors. Now much of that rediscovered heritage has been lost for ever.

This picture of the ancient citadel, Arg-e-Bam, was taken just a few months before the earthquake. The citadel dated from the tenth century and was the largest example of mud-brick architecture in the world. Attempts are now being made to restore it.

Lasting effects

Many local people, traumatized by the deaths of so many members of their families, have lost the will to rebuild their lives. Some have turned to drugs as an escape. Others have left to live with relatives in other parts of the country. Recovery is slow. As with all major disasters, the physical and mental scars will remain for a very long time. What is certain is that the historic city of Bam will never be the same again.

EYEWITNESS

❝ The new design will have to take into account proper seismic design techniques. When you go with old-style engineering, you're looking for trouble so we're going to change it now. ❞

Dr. Hamid Eskander, Head of Bam reconstruction

PAKISTAN AND KASHMIR, 2005

On October 8, 2005, at 8:52 a.m., a massive earthquake struck near the town of Muzaffarabad in Kashmir, 50 miles (80 km) northeast of the Pakistani capital, Islamabad. Kashmir is a disputed region of the Indian subcontinent, part controlled by India and part by Pakistan. The earthquake's epicenter was almost exactly on the border between the two countries. The earthquake was so huge that it affected large areas of India, Pakistan, and Afghanistan.

Massive impact

The earthquake measured 7.6 on the Richter scale and was followed by 140 aftershocks. It devastated communities far and wide. The mountainous and inaccessible terrain, and the cruel winter weather, worsened the disaster and increased the death toll. Rescue teams found it difficult to reach the many isolated villages that were shaken to the ground. More than a year after the event, thousands of people were still living in temporary shelters in the harshest of conditions. Many had suffered a second, freezing winter in isolated locations.

EYEWITNESS

❝ I want to go back to the old days, but I know that's impossible. God gave me my son. God took him away again. It's as if someone has ripped my heart out. ❞

Rubi Noreen, survivor, Balakot

Rubi's story

At 8:52 a.m. on the day of the earthquake, Rubi Noreen was walking home after taking her six-year-old son to school in Balakot, 19 miles (30 km) northwest of the epicenter. A building collapsed on her, crushing her right leg. She was buried under rubble for six hours before rescuers dug her out. It was another five days before they found the body of her son in the wreckage of his school. Rubi's comfortable home was destroyed, killing her two sisters and a brother. Barely a building in the entire town, built on the sides of a steep mountain valley, was left standing.

More than a year later, Rubi was still living beneath a flimsy shelter made of tarpaulins and plastic sheeting on the foundations of what used to be her home. Her leg, swollen and yellow, was encased in a caliper (brace). She was still unable to walk.

A boy stands on the remains of his house in the town of Balakot. Despite wire reinforcements, the concrete ceilings have completely collapsed.

GHOST TOWN

Not a single building of two or more stories remains in Balakot. As many as 8,000 out of 40,000 inhabitants died in the disaster— many of them children. Balakot is unlikely ever to be rebuilt. It sits almost exactly on the fault line that created the disaster. The Pakistani government plans to rebuild the town about 12 miles (20 km) away. But Rubi, like many of the other inhabitants, does not want to leave. Many generations of her family have lived and died here. Now the grave of her son is here, too.

The bigger picture

Rubi's story is just one among tens of thousands. So what about the bigger picture? The damage caused by the earthquake covered a vast area. A staggering 1,000 hospitals alone were destroyed, along with more than 6,000 schools and colleges. Thousands of mountain villages were cut off. By October 12, 2005, 23,000 people had been declared dead but the death toll would rise much higher. Fears of widespread disease were voiced amid the desperate conditions.

Yet, although cases of gangrene (caused by the infection of untreated wounds) and other illnesses such as diarrhea were reported, the threatened epidemic did not happen. Perhaps the cold weather contributed to this—diseases such as cholera tend to spread more easily in hot, tropical climates. Perhaps just as surprisingly, the United Nations reported no cases of malnutrition (caused by insufficient or poor-quality food), even though six of the nine districts affected were areas where food is traditionally in short supply. In reaction to the disaster, over 200,000 tons of food were given to over two million people, including 745,000 people stranded in inaccessible mountainous locations.

EYEWITNESS

❝ There will be no fresh water and no food. Our fear is that diseases such as cholera will take hold as people become desperate. The risk is that they will have to drink contaminated water. Medical help is needed if the situation is not going to get worse. ❞

Leyla Berlement, International Committee of the Red Cross

Survivors huddle on a remote mountainside in Jabla, Kashmir. Hypothermia was a threat since people were stranded in the cold for long periods, waiting for aid and shelter.

Pakistani soldiers distribute aid in Bagh city, Kashmir. The provision of basic supplies, such as clean drinking water, is essential if people are to survive in the immediate aftermath of an earthquake.

The political dimension

The disputed area in which the Kashmir earthquake occurred has a history of tension and conflict. If ever there was a time for India and Pakistan to put aside their differences, then this was surely it. And in many ways, that is what happened. On October 18, Pervez Musharraf, the president of Pakistan, proposed to open up what is known as the Line of Control, a boundary that divides the two sides of the disputed territory. This would enable military forces from both sides, as well as aid agencies, to reach isolated places more easily. Both India and the international community welcomed the move.

However, cooperation was not as total as some would have liked. President Musharraf had already refused help from Indian helicopters in Pakistan-controlled Kashmir. He was concerned that these might be used to gain information about the region. Others dismissed this idea as ridiculous in the face of such a terrible disaster. These are difficult issues to address, especially when a government believes its national security is at stake. Even so, most observers agree that cooperation between the two countries has been generally good in the aftermath of the earthquake, and some of the worst fears of conflict have been avoided.

QUAKE COSTS

- 87,350 deaths
- 3,300,000 people made homeless
- Total cost: around $21 billion

The road to recovery

Rebuilding the affected parts of Kashmir and Pakistan is an enormous job. Some progress has been made in bringing relief to those who survived the earthquake. In Balakot, for example, a bridge has been repaired and huge quantities of rubble have been cleared. Huts and tents that serve as schools and clinics have been erected by the many aid agencies with bases around the town. But work has started on only a fraction of the 600,000 homes that need to be replaced across the disaster region. President Musharraf promised that the rebuilding program would be complete by 2008. In reality, it is likely to take five years longer.

REBUILDING LIVES

Almost a million tents were distributed following the earthquake, along with millions of sheets of plastic to protect the tents from rain and snow. Authorities set up 12 housing reconstruction centers to help train people to rebuild their homes. More than 75,000 people have been given basic training. The United Nations allocated $100 million for 26 programs involving seed distribution, fertilizers, livestock, and agricultural training.

Government help

After the disaster, people who had lost their homes were offered a grant of 150,000 rupees ($2,500) by a World Bank-funded government scheme to rebuild their homes. Those with partially damaged houses were offered 50,000 rupees (about $830). The government insisted, however, that new houses should be made of cement and steel to make them earthquake resistant.

The high cost of buying and transporting materials unfortunately meant that many homes were started but not finished, partly because the grants were paid only in instalments. Wood has now been suggested as an alternative building material. Many homeowners were unable to provide proof of ownership, and many of the survivors had been landless even before the earthquake and so could not get compensation. For the time being at least, many people have had to build temporary shelters out of the ruins of their flattened communities.

Uncertain future

Despite the almost overwhelming difficulties, many reports suggest that the Pakistani authorities did well to prevent more deaths from exposure and disease during the winter a year after the earthquake. With international help, the government has set up temporary schools and hospitals, some of which are better than those destroyed. But the suffering continues and enormous problems remain. As is so often the case with natural disasters, the survivors show great courage in the face of adversity. However, they know that the future is uncertain.

Life goes on in Balakot. Despite the devastation, an enterprising villager sets up a shop among the ruins.

Learning the lessons

Part of a seismologist's work is to study what causes earthquakes and to try to find ways of predicting when they are likely to happen. Scientists are also improving methods of protecting people when these unavoidable natural disasters occur.

BRIGHT LIGHTS

In Tangshan, China, in 1976, residents were woken one night by fireballs and flashes in the sky. The following night, an earthquake registering 7.8 on the Richter scale killed nearly a quarter of a million people. Could the two events have been connected? This was not the first time people had seen strange light effects before a quake. One theory is that the immense stresses generated in rocks before an earthquake can give off energy in the form of light or heat.

Predicting earthquakes

Many earthquake-prone parts of the world are now wired up with complex arrays of detectors, which trace patterns of seismic activity. Seismic patterns can also sometimes be recorded over many years and used as a basis for predictions. Checking water levels and the buildup of some gases, and monitoring low-frequency radio waves, have been tried as additional methods of quake prediction. In 2007–8, scientists on board a colossal ship will attempt to drill 22,960 ft. (7,000 m) into an oceanic plate, straight into a subduction zone. They hope this will uncover seismic information that may help to indicate when an earthquake is due. But nothing has yet proved fully reliable at predicting the time, place, or intensity of the next major earthquake.

These "lo-tech" earthquake-proof homes have been built to house poor communities in Manizales, Colombia. Creating more stable buildings does not always mean having to find expensive solutions. Design features may include hollow concrete bricks and steel corner pillars to provide both strength and flexibility.

Making buildings safer

Throughout this book, we have seen examples of how better building techniques and designs could save thousands of people from being crushed to death. The world's tallest building, Taipei 101 in Taiwan, is an example of this. It is supported by "dog bone" steel beams designed to stretch at narrow points in the center and absorb any shock away from the welding at the end of the beams where they might snap. But solutions such as this are expensive and hi-tech. They do not meet the needs of millions of poor people living in crowded conditions in earthquake danger zones. Simpler methods, such as linking traditional straw-brick houses together with wire and bamboo struts, can help improve stability. More techniques like this need to be adopted, or huge populations will remain at risk.

A final lesson?

The science of earthquake prediction is improving all the time, and much can be done to make buildings safer worldwide. But we also have to recognize that the force of nature is vast, dangerous, and unpredictable. We have to learn how to manage it the best we can.

BUILDING WORKS

Before the Bam disaster (pages 32–37), two other Iranian cities, Golbaf and Ghaen, were hit by earthquakes, reconstructed, and then hit a second time. More than 1,500 people were killed when the second quake struck Ghaen. But in Golbaf, an equally strong quake caused just five deaths. In both cases, houses had been designed to withstand earthquakes. The difference was that in Golbaf, careful workmanship and supervision meant that houses had been built to the right standards.

Education is an important aspect of disaster protection. These Japanese employees are learning first aid in a disaster prevention drill near Tokyo, part of a mass program across the country.

Glossary

aftershock Ground shaking caused by underground rocks repositioning after an earthquake.

building regulations Codes that are designed to ensure high standards of building construction but often ignored or bypassed, particularly in poorer regions.

cholera A potentially fatal disease, carried in water polluted by human waste. Cholera causes severe dehydration (see below).

convection currents Movements of liquids or gases caused when heated, less dense matter rises and cooler, denser matter sinks.

debris Scattered material, such as tree branches or building rubble, that has been dislodged or broken and left behind after an earthquake or other disaster.

dehydration Low water levels in the body, caused by a shortage of drinking water or as a result of severe vomiting or diarrhea.

epicenter The point on the Earth's surface immediately above an earthquake, from which waves and tremors radiate outward.

fault line A line of weakness in rocks, usually occurring along the boundary between two tectonic plates and along which earthquakes are likely to occur.

focus The point below the Earth's surface, within the crust, at which an earthquake or tremor originates.

foundations The underground structure that supports a building.

frequency The rate at which something shakes, for example, during an earthquake, measured in vibrations per second.

geology The composition and structure of rocks and soils in a particular area.

hypothermia An abnormal lowering of body temperature, which can endanger life.

infrastructure Things built for services and communications, such as roads, telephone and electricity cables, and water pipes.

landslide The sudden movement of a mass of soil and rocks down a slope.

liquefaction When soils are subjected to severe vibration and begin to behave like a liquid, causing buildings to sink.

prefabricated Made in sections that can be easily transported and assembled on site.

resonance When vibrations (or tremors) of similar frequency build on each other, greatly increasing the overall vibration.

retrofitting The system of modifying or strengthening existing buildings and other structures to make them more resistant to disasters such as earthquakes.

Richter scale A system used to measure and compare the strength of earthquakes.

seismic Relates to earth movements and all aspects of the study of earthquakes.

shock absorbers Building features that can resist shocks, reducing the risk of collapse.

subduction When the edge of one tectonic plate slides beneath another.

tectonic plates Giant sections into which the Earth's crust is divided and which move slowly in relation to each other, giving rise to earthquakes and other natural hazards.

tremors The surface vibrations experienced after an earthquake.

tsunami A series of waves at sea, caused by an undersea earthquake, landslide, or volcanic explosion.

vibrations Shaking or trembling.

World Bank An international organization that lends money to poorer nations to help their development or to enable them to recover more rapidly from natural disasters.

Further Information

Books

Earth Shaking Science: What We Know (And Don't Know) About Earthquakes
Elizabeth Hough, Princeton University Press, 2004

Natural Disasters (DK Eyewitness Books)
Claire Watts, DK Children, 2006

Natural Disasters (Kingfisher Knowledge)
Andrew Langley, Kingfisher, 2006

Natural Disasters: Earthquakes
Allison Lassieur, Capstone Press, 2003

Violent Volcanoes and Earth-shattering Earthquakes (Horrible Geography)
Anita Ganeri and Mike Phillips,
Scholastic, 2006

Web Sites

Due to the changing nature of Internet links, Rosen Publishing has developed an online list of Web sites related to the subject of this book. This site is regularly updated. Please use this link to access this list:
http://www.rosenlinks.com/nda/eaia

Index